Self and Career Advancement

Self and Career Advancement

Phoenix Rivers

CONTENTS

Chapter 1: Introduction

This book is designed to help you reflect on your attitude, self-image, values, vision, and goals for your future success. We have crafted a set of key questions to assist you in this reflection, enabling growth in both your personal and professional life. These questions are designed to provoke deep thought and help you identify practices and methods that will aid your career growth.

Each of the following descriptions offers the potential for profound transformation, helping you reach the success you have been longing for. Take your time to consider these questions carefully, as they are essential for your self and career advancement. Are you prepared to take an honest look at yourself and your professional aspirations?

These questions are grouped into themes to help you explore different aspects of your life and career. They are designed to fulfill the desires, dreams, and hopes that still burn within you, turning your professional aspirations into reality. These twelve key questions have been meticulously crafted to bring about deep, meaningful change and propel you towards success.

Purpose and Scope of the Book

The purpose of this book is to provide individuals with the tools needed for personal and professional development and career advancement through self-reflection. In today's rapidly changing world, professionals are constantly seeking resources to aid in their development. This book addresses the needs in personal development and career advancement by posing insightful questions about the self.

This section offers a brief overview of the book, its objectives, scope, and value proposition. It outlines the structure and contents of the book, providing you with a roadmap for your journey of self-discovery and professional growth.

Self and Career Advancement: Transformation Through Self-Questions

The aim of this book is to enable personal and professional growth through self-reflection. By posing twelve insightful questions, the book encourages you to look inward, dig deep, and work through your unique situations. This process of self-transformation will empower you to take control of your life and manage your career more effectively.

The book is divided into six parts, each containing two chapters. As you delve into this book, be prepared to face many challenging questions. This discomfort is a natural and necessary part of the growth process. The questions may be difficult to answer for various reasons: you may not know the answers, you may be reluctant to admit certain truths, or the issues may be deeply personal. It's essential to approach these questions with an open mind and a willingness to engage in soul-searching work.

To get the most out of this book, set aside a large chunk of time to ponder these questions in one sitting. This will allow you to uncover honest and real solutions about who you are and what you want from life. Treat each question with the respect it deserves, and let this journey of self-discovery transform your professional and personal life.

Chapter 2: Understanding Self

Understanding the Self

Self is the core of one's existence. It is the first and last point of reference, influencing all actions and inactions. Without a clear and factual understanding of this 'self,' achieving meaningful transformation can be challenging. Financial success is often seen as straightforward, but delving into the 'intrapsychic' aspects of oneself is crucial for attaining personal and career growth.

Understanding fundamental questions like "Who are you?", "Why are you?", and "What are you?" plays a critical role in self-awareness. In today's world, self-awareness is essential for personal and career growth. Transforming oneself and gaining a clear understanding are profound endeavors.

1. **Who are you?**
2. **Why are you?** (Understanding the essence of your existence)
3. **What are you doing here?** (Defining your purpose)
4. **What can you afford?** (Exploring your capabilities and objectivity)
5. **How can you create your life as a work of art?** (Envisioning your future)

Question 1: What are my core values and beliefs?

There are twelve key questions to help you grow and transform your inner self and career. The first question is: **What are your core values and beliefs?** Reflect on your core beliefs and values and the formative experiences that shaped them. Core values guide our vision and actions, underlying why we do things the way we do. Life revolves around embracing certain values and rejecting others.

In your journey of self-discovery, one of the biggest tasks is discerning what you care about most and living by those values every day. Core values prompt questions like: "Whom do I want to be in my everyday life?" "What principles are irreplaceable to me?" and "What resonates with my inner self?" These answers reveal fundamental truths about who we are, our purpose, what brings joy and happiness, and what sustains us through life's challenges.

Reflect on your life, career, relationships, and experiences to identify patterns or significant moments that signify what has always been most meaningful to you. This question opens a journey down memory lane, uncovering the essence of your values.

Question 2: What are my strengths and areas for growth?

We all have unique skills, abilities, and knowledge. However, research suggests that many people are not fully aware of their true strengths. It is common, particularly among women, to understate their abilities or feel uncomfortable highlighting what they do well. Recognizing and appreciating your strengths is crucial as they offer opportunities for career development.

At the same time, it is essential to realistically assess areas for growth. Undertaking a full skill or competency assessment with a qualified professional can provide an unbiased view of your strengths and areas for improvement. Staying in your comfort zone for too long can hinder continuous learning and development.

Therefore, consider new roles or routes where there are further opportunities for skill application and growth.

Question 3: What motivates and energizes me?

Motivators are things that hold special meaning for us. Our values and personal beliefs drive our internal motivation system. Positive and negative triggers can induce emotional responses, prompting us to take action. This emotional response creates or triggers motivation, passion, enthusiasm, and drive.

When you are aligned with your highest ideals, you feel purposeful, clear, authentic, focused, and driven. This energy comes from within and is evident even if not explicitly asked for by others. Our energy sources lie primarily in the expressive and motivational domains of our emotional state. You know you are tapping into your energy source when you feel passionate, alive, and enthusiastic.

Questions about motivators help identify your highest personal values, such as what is most important to you at this stage in your life or career. Identifying your passions and enthusiasms reveals where your energy and drive lie.

Question 4: How do I handle challenges and setbacks?

Handling challenges and setbacks effectively is crucial for personal and professional growth. Whether you take calculated risks or play it safe, adopt strategies that allow you to cope with future uncertainties. Not all coping strategies are equally effective. Some, like anger suppression or inauthentic coping, can backfire.

Consider developmental-stage coping training or addressing foundational belief systems behind your coping strategies through professional assistance for long-lasting benefits. Resilience, defined as the ability to successfully combat adversity, is vital. Key resilience factors include:

- Nurturing meaningful and reliable personal relationships

- Perceiving oneself as strong and capable
- Developing a confidence-enhancing view of oneself as competent
- Being problem-focused and viewing challenges as solvable

Effectiveness in handling challenges involves mobilizing thoughts and behaviors to respond rationally and flexibly to obstacles. Develop a strategy that reflects your self, career, and situation, which can be implemented and adapted as needed. Adaptivity is essential in overcoming life's challenges.

Chapter 3: Setting Goals and Vision

Are you setting goals for your life that are strong enough to help transform you into the person you'd like to become? Only by envisioning who you want to be and what you want to achieve can you accomplish the kind of spectacular success that can transform your life. Many people live their lives in quiet desperation, devoid of vision or goals. If they have a goal, it is usually for temporary enrichment, like making a lot of money quickly.

In thinking about what you want to do and who you want to become, you might start by thinking broadly and implementing long-range goals as described by Brian Tracy. Ask yourself: What would you like to accomplish during your career and life? Whether it's one year or ten years from now, what experiences from both your professional and personal life do you want to look back on with pride? What do you want to be admired for or known as? When managers interview you and ask this question in conjunction with the life you want to have, they are not just distinguishing whether you are materialistic or would make "sound" career choices. They are using this information to get a sense of your self-image, the amount of initiative and creativity you possess, and ultimately, your level of ambition.

Question 5: Where do I see myself in the next 5 years?

This question entails envisioning what your career may look like in the next five years. It requires considerable thought and insightful consideration. Five years can be a very long time, especially when looking back. What did you think your career would look like five years ago? Are you doing the same thing, or have you transformed and developed into something else? How did that happen?

Strategic thinking involves considering outcomes and tracing them back to the present. While no one can predict the future, successful people often have a vision and a strategic plan. They create a roadmap of possibilities. During job interviews, you are often asked where you see yourself in five years. This encourages you to think about where your career is headed. Planning for the long-term commitment needed and expected in a position ties into strategic planning and long-term vision. Thinking strategically makes life exciting, allowing you to determine where you want to go and how to get there.

Question 6: What are my short-term and long-term career goals?

The process of self-inquiry and reflection should create fertile ground for your unconscious mind to grow and germinate answers and solutions to your career advancement questions. As you consider each of the twelve career advancement questions, know that your true nature and values may not be perfectly defined and will evolve over time. That's okay. We come to know ourselves through this open and honest process.

Question six: What are my short-term and long-term career goals? Some job seekers have difficulty envisioning their career five years from now. The question becomes less intimidating if you break it down into smaller sections. Think about where you'd like to be in six weeks. Then, consider accomplishing that goal and defining your priorities for the next six months. Continue this process until you reach a five-year goal that feels logical to you.

Your goal doesn't have to be extremely specific. Since your ultimate objective will likely alter as you progress, concentrate on the next several steps you'll need to take. Make these milestones specific and manageable. Commit to taking small, positive actions to assist you in reaching your long-term career goals. Once you've established your major objectives, break them down further into the steps needed to reach them.

Chapter 4: Building Skills and Knowledge

Building Skills and Knowledge

Success in today's rapidly changing world requires self-expression and the ethos of continuous learning. Embracing continuous learning opens us to new possibilities, helps establish broad and diverse networks, and encourages investment in our energy, time, talents, happiness, and inner growth. Skills and knowledge have a unique characteristic: when you invest in them, they're yours forever. You don't lose them if your job changes. In fact, being skillful becomes your most important asset for getting ahead and staying ahead.

Experience today will help you develop the skills to take on increasingly important responsibilities. Understanding power dynamics is crucial for building your influence, which requires extensive knowledge. In today's competitive environment, employers and business clients only want to work with the best of the best.

To improve your career advancement prospects, hiring managers want to know your accomplishments, work ethic, communication skills, and more. In other words, they want the whole package. Possessing the necessary competencies may lead to promotions or more responsible roles. Competencies are categorized into three areas:

knowledge development and application, general business aptitude, and formal education. You must possess and exhibit these abilities in a modern and powerful work environment. These skills must also be continually developed, strengthened, and updated throughout your career.

Question 7: What new skills do I want to acquire?

One key question to ask yourself is: **What new skills do I want to acquire?** Identify the skills and knowledge gaps that need to be filled to become the manager or employee you aspire to be. Compare the skills you currently have with those needed to succeed in your desired role.

Consider the skills necessary for the work you want to do and whether they can be achieved using available technology. The skills identified through this comparison can guide your career path and help you get ahead.

To acquire professional abilities, it may be efficient to talk with professional business partners, managers, and supervisors about training opportunities. If direct discussion isn't possible, explore your company's procedures for a "training and development plan." Identify potential skills to acquire, gain training in your field, increase competency in your role, and gain the technology needed for your career progression. Look for existing training programs that can aid your growth, and explore potential matches or create a profile to assess your suitability for various vocations.

Question 8: How can I enhance my existing skills?

When contemplating self-improvement for a career move or job opportunity, it is common to focus on areas lacking talent or competencies. While addressing these gaps is important, self-progression often emphasizes maximizing effectiveness and efficiency. Instead of starting from scratch, use your existing learning and experience as a foundation to refine and expand.

Reflect on your past achievements and skills. Consider acquiring new skills that build upon these areas of expertise. This disciplined method allows you to leverage what you already have to offer.

Invest time in cultivating, upgrading, and growing your established skills. Determine whether your learning is aligned with the standards of formal coordinating bodies in your sector or business. Start by reviewing relevant professional journals and their specialties. Consider technological developments that may impact your field. Study your abilities through round tables, case studies, and beyond. Your expertise forms the cornerstone of formal appraisal systems. Interview your supervisor for feedback and put your skills to the test in both leadership and technical capacities.

Chapter 5: Networking and Relationships

Research demonstrates the value of your network as a measure of essential career capital. By examining the career of Sven Borg, a successful CEO, we can see real-life networking in action. Networking and relationships are common terms used to describe human social interactions. People use these words in networking events, casual chats, interviews, career counseling sessions, and mentoring circles. However, these are profoundly significant terms based on sociological concepts of coalitions, alliances, dyads, and power relationships. Tending personal connections and forming coalitions is a part of social life. Applying these underlying ideas purposefully and imaginatively in your life embodies transformational living.

People often recommend focusing on career development by connecting with as many "right" contacts (superiors and senior people in your business) as possible and attending the "right" networking activities. Seeking a mentor is also highly valued, as mentors can provide wisdom, knowledge, and access to important connections. Mentors are essential in a learning partnership, which should begin as an intrinsically motivated relationship. Modern networking is less about finding new jobs and more about learning and progressing personal and career changes. A mentor may appear unexpectedly during this networking process, offering support due to shared goals and a strong learning relationship.

Question 9: Who are my mentors and role models?

If you're not actively building mentor relationships, you might find yourself feeling isolated. Chances are, you don't have a mentor, and even if you do, you might not be engaging with them regularly. Effective mentors help others develop quickly, and it's wise to seek counsel from others. You can improve your performance as a mentor as well.

Role models provide powerful inspiration for personal transformation. Reflecting on who your role models are can guide your growth. Finding a mentor can be challenging, but those dedicated to self-improvement and understanding the need for help often succeed. Look for people who exhibit qualities you admire and frequently ask for guidance. Establish connections with those who are world-class in the areas you want to grow in and seek their support.

Question 10: How can I expand my professional network?

Career advancement requires knowing the right people, and networking doesn't just happen—it requires proactive steps. Here are some strategies to expand your professional network:

- **Research trade and industry associations:** Identify those relevant to your work and career. These associations often have local and regional chapters that can provide networking opportunities.
- **Join social networking sites:** Create an online profile on LinkedIn and connect with current and former colleagues. Use your LinkedIn profile URL in your email signature or on business cards to direct people to your profile.

- **Reconnect with former contacts:** Search for former customers, clients, and fellow employees online. Reach out to them and reshape past business relationships.
- **Contact college alumni associations:** If you've moved to a new city, connect with local or national alumni chapters. For a fee, you can obtain contact information for alumni in your area and invite them to meet for coffee or lunch.
- **Join service organizations or sports leagues:** Participate in groups like the Rotary Club, Lions Club, or PTA to meet people. Build relationships by encouraging others and volunteering in these organizations. Participate in single-day service projects to meet new people and showcase your value as a potential employee.

Chapter 6: Overcoming Obstacles

Success is rarely linear, nor is it often solitary. Many who seek to advance their personal and career growth quickly encounter obstacles. This is an almost inevitable aspect of trying to grow or change—advancement requires overcoming challenges. Opponents of growth can come from anywhere. Sometimes, it's our own fears and doubts that drag us down or hold us back. Other times, it's the less-than-supportive attitudes of others that divert our focus from our real goals. By acknowledging these challenges, you can mentally prepare to embrace the effort it takes to overcome them. Life will be difficult at times, but from these difficulties will spring resilience, creativity, and curiosity, ultimately making it worth the effort.

Challenges will come, and slip-ups will occur. Mistakes and resistance are part of the journey. When you encounter bumps in the road, don't see them as wasted effort. Instead, use difficult experiences to guide your future approach. If your schedule gets busier and you struggle to maintain your self-development routine, find solutions that allow you to adapt. Missed opportunities or time spent on an unfulfilling career path can guide your future decisions. Reflect on what you disliked about previous paths and identify opportunities in your chosen career to apply your skills. Grow your skillset to ensure you are ready for future opportunities.

Question 11: What fears or self-limiting beliefs hold me back?

We all have fears and self-limiting beliefs stemming from past experiences. Yet, if not confronted, these fears can become personal barriers. Identifying the source of your fear helps to bring it down to earth. Confronting the fear, even from a distance, can diminish its power. Fear of failure is one of the most common fears. What are you afraid of? Why? Is it realistic, or are you preparing for the worst?

Identify ways in which you have limited yourself. How have you held yourself back or denied yourself important aspects of life? Reflecting on these concepts and showing yourself compassion can reduce distress and build confidence. How do these limitations affect your personal and professional growth? What steps have you taken or will you take to overcome your fears and self-restraints?

Speak to trusted individuals to get feedback on whether your perceived hurdles are average, uncommon, or transcendent.

Question 12: How can I overcome obstacles and setbacks?

The old saying "when the going gets tough, the tough get going" may be clichéd but holds a ring of truth. Obstacles and setbacks are inevitable parts of life. You can't avoid them or dodge most of them. The world is designed to be a big obstacle course, challenging us to face and deal with insecurities and uneasiness. This process helps us learn problem-solving, decisive action, and overcoming adversity.

You must accept this reality both cognitively and emotionally. Cognitive acceptance involves rational acknowledgment of truth, while emotional acceptance brings inner peace. Adaptive problem-solving is essential, avoiding experiential avoidance. Confronting trauma and finding coping mechanisms helps prevent emotional displacement.

Studies show that individuals who initiate problem-solving strategies during stress are less susceptible to depression. Adaptable individuals avoid rigidity and embrace flexibility. Overcoming obstacles involves destroying barriers, not self-esteem. Achieving excellence requires conquering challenges and "colonizers of the mind." Success is not easy, and our drive to cope with obstacles etches out character. Developing effective coping mechanisms is essential.

Chapter 7: Conclusion

In conclusion, this book is a guide to self-discovery and transformation through critical reflective questions and journaling. The twelve questions presented in this book can be used to transform any aspect of your life and career. We suggest starting with self-discovery. Following some answers and personal transformation, you can then uncover your personal brand, mission, ethics, and career goals. Spend time and resources seeking fulfilling work, entrepreneurship, or volunteer opportunities. Few questionnaires rival the impact of these transformational questions.

This work provides insight into the remarkable benefits of critically examining your career and life through revealing questions. Undertaking this type of challenge can lead to professional and mental growth, helping you better understand yourself and become more career resilient in these unpredictable times. Focusing on marketing and promotion can increase the reach of subsequent career guidance workshops and coaching consultancy outputs, making the financial investment worthwhile. We hope this chapter encourages our peers to take a more critical look at their career development needs, seeking answers to transformational changes in the deep identity foundations of the individual. In this way, the philosophical roots of this work may continue beyond our practice-based evidence.

Key Takeaways and Action Steps

Key takeaways: One of Plumtree's chief insights as we discussed our plans was the word "trusting." This book is about building trust, a critical dimension in these challenging times. For your own learning and reflection, re-read the personal and career development sections through the lens of trust.

So, what are we left with? We have had a powerful conversation, drawing on the wisdom of well-known and respected scholar-practitioners in the fields of career performance, management, innovation, and learning. As my wise father-in-law advises, "So, what are you going to do now?" Here are a dozen "now-next" actions to fuel your development in positive, meaningful ways and mirror your impact in the workplace:

1. Re-read the "Key Insights and Applications" section to the very left.
2. Select something from groupings A, B, and C that energizes and interests you and is within your sphere of influence to act upon (mental reminder: you don't need to take on "world peace" all at once).
3. Consider sharing the question you select to explore in a small group or one-on-one for feedback and support. If you can't find any "live" others, consider posting your question in our online "virtual gathering" to see what the expansive group thinks.
4. Put the modeling example to work for you. If we suggested an approach for modeling the various forms "ownership" might take, consider applying this to your change project.

5. Enjoy the powerful conversations and ideas that will emerge for you!

9 798330 587971